PITTSBURGH
STEELERS

BY JOSH ANDERSON

Stride

An Imprint of The Child's World®

childsworld.com

The
Child's
World.
childsworld.com

Published by The Child's World®
800-599-READ • www.childsworld.com

Photography Credits
Cover: © Justin K. Aller / Stringer / Getty Images; page 1: © Africa Studio / Shutterstock; page 3: © Katharine Lotze / Staff / Getty Images; page 5: © Justin K. Aller / Stringer / Getty Images; page 6: © SportsChrom / Newscom; page 9: © Jonathan Daniel / Staff / Getty Images; page 10: © Michael Heiman / Staff / Getty Images; page 11: © stevezmina1 / Getty Images; page 12: © Joe Sargent / Stringer / Getty Images; page 12: © Frederick Breedon / Stringer / Getty Images; page 13: © "Ai Wire Photo Service" / Newscom; page 13: © Gregory Shamus / Stringer / Getty Images; page 14: © Justin Berl / Stringer / Getty Images; page 15: © Jason Merritt / Stringer / Getty Images; page 16: © / Dreamstime; page 16: © Chuck Solomon/Icon SMI / Newscom; page 17: © SportsChrome / Newscom; page 17: © Matt Sullivan / Stringer / Getty Images; page 18: © PM / SportsChrome / Newscom; page 18: © Vernon Biever / Associated Press; page 19: © Tony Tomsic / SportsChrome / Newscom; page 19: © Brian Bahr / Staff / Getty Images; page 20: © Joe Sargent / Stringer / Getty Images; page 20: © Emilee Chinn / Stringer / Getty Images; page 20: © Joe Sargent / Stringer / Getty Images; page 21: © Joe Sargent / Stringer / Getty Images; page 22: © PM / SportsChrome / Newscom; page 23: © Ezra Shaw / Staff / Getty Images; page 23: © stevezmina1 / Getty Images; page 25: © Chris McGrath / Staff / Getty Images; page 26: © Elsa / Staff / Getty Images; page 29: © Gregory Shamus / Stringer / Getty Images

ISBN Information
9781503857681 (Reinforced Library Binding)
9781503860643 (Portable Document Format)
9781503862005 (Online Multi-user eBook)
9781503863361 (Electronic Publishing)

LCCN 2021952639

Printed in the United States of America

TABLE OF CONTENTS

GO STEELERS!

The Pittsburgh Steelers compete in the National Football **League's** (NFL's) American Football Conference (AFC). They play in the AFC North **division**, along with the Baltimore Ravens, Cincinnati Bengals, and Cleveland Browns. Fans in Pittsburgh have been lucky! The Steelers have won the **Super Bowl** six times. They are tied with the New England Patriots for the most Super Bowl wins. Let's learn more about the Steelers!

AFC NORTH DIVISION

Baltimore Ravens

Cincinnati Bengals

Cleveland Browns

Pittsburgh Steelers

ROOKIES NAJEE HARRIS AND PAT FREIERMUTH ADDED A NEW DIMENSION TO THE STEELERS OFFENSE IN 2021.

BECOMING THE STEELERS

The team began play in 1933 as the Pittsburgh Pirates. That's the same name as the city's Major League Baseball (MLB) team. Pittsburgh, Pennsylvania, is a city that once produced a large amount of the steel used in the United States. In 1940, the team adopted the name "Steelers" to represent the city's major industry. In their first 37 seasons, the Steelers made the **playoffs** only one time. But since 1972, the Steelers have made the postseason more often than they have not.

QUARTERBACK TERRY BRADSHAW STARTED 158 GAMES FOR THE STEELERS DURING HIS 14-YEAR CAREER.

BY THE NUMBERS

The Steelers have won **SIX** Super Bowls.

25 division titles for the Steelers

436 points for the team in 2014—a Steelers record!

15 wins for the Steelers in 2004

THE STEELERS' VICTORY IN SUPER BOWL 40 EARNED THE TEAM ITS FIRST CHAMPIONSHIP IN MORE THAN 25 YEARS.

THE STEELERS HAVE WON EIGHT PLAYOFF GAMES AT HEINZ FIELD.

The Steelers have had several homes throughout their history. Their first home **stadium** was Forbes Field, where they played until 1963. From 1970 until 2000, they played in Three Rivers Stadium, which was also home to MLB's Pittsburgh Pirates. Since 2001, the team has called Heinz Field its home. About 68,000 fans can fit inside Heinz Field to root for the Steelers at home games. Every seat has been sold for every Steelers home game since 1972.

We're Famous!

A bunch of Steelers appear in a scene from the 2012 Batman film *The Dark Knight Rises*, which was shot at Heinz Field in Pittsburgh. Quarterback Ben Roethlisberger, wide receiver Hines Ward, and several other Steelers play members of the fictional Gotham Rogues football team. Their game is interrupted by the film's villain, Bane. Too bad Batman wasn't around at the moment to keep the game moving forward.

UNIFORM

BLACK

WHITE

Truly Weird

The Steelers trailed 7–6 in the final minute of a 1972 playoff game. Steelers quarterback Terry Bradshaw heaved a long pass toward running back John Fuqua. As the ball arrived, it bounced off either Fuqua's hands or a defender's helmet. The ball then sailed about ten yards through the air, where it was caught by Steelers running back Franco Harris. Harris ran 60 yards for the **touchdown**, and the Steelers won the game 13–7. The play has been nicknamed the "Immaculate Reception" because it was such an unlikely catch.

Alternate Jersey

Sometimes teams wear an alternate jersey that is different from their home and away jerseys. It might be a bright color or have a unique theme. For a 2016 game against the New York Jets, the Steelers wore striped uniforms similar to the ones they wore during their first season ever in 1933. The new-but-old look proved lucky: the Steelers won the game.

FANS IN PITTSBURGH HAVE BEEN WAVING "TERRIBLE TOWELS" SINCE 1975 TO CHEER ON THE STEELERS. THE YELLOW TOWELS ARE MUST-HAVE ITEMS FOR FANS AT HEINZ FIELD.

Going to a game at Heinz Field can be a blast. Fans create a sea of yellow by waving their "terrible towels" in unison to cheer on the Steelers. Fans chant, "Here we go, Steelers" throughout the game to inspire the players. In 1961, the Steelers became one of the first NFL teams to have its own cheerleading squad. But the Pittsburgh Steelerettes disbanded in 1969, and the team hasn't had cheerleaders since. The team's mascot is Steely McBeam. He's a costumed man wearing a hard hat and overalls. He's inspired by the city's history in the steelmaking industry.

STEELY MCBEAM

HEROES OF HISTORY

Mel Blount
Cornerback | 1970–1983

Blount's 57 career interceptions are tied for 13th in NFL history. His interception in Super Bowl 9 helped lead the Steelers to one of their four championships during his career. He's a member of the Pro Football **Hall of Fame**. Blount was also picked for the NFL's 100th Anniversary All-Time Team.

Terry Bradshaw
Quarterback | 1970–1983

Bradshaw led the Steelers to four Super Bowl victories during his career. He led the league in passing touchdowns twice. In 1978, he was chosen as the NFL's **Most Valuable Player** (MVP). He was chosen for three **Pro Bowls** and is a member of the Pro Football Hall of Fame.

Jack Lambert
Linebacker | 1974–1984

One of the game's greatest tacklers, Lambert helped lead the Steelers to four Super Bowl victories. Lambert was chosen as the NFL's Defensive Player of the Year in 1976. He was also picked for nine Pro Bowls. He's in the Hall of Fame and is also a member of the NFL's 100th Anniversary All-Time Team.

Hines Ward
Wide Receiver | 1998–2011

Ward's 12,083 yards and 85 receiving touchdowns are Steelers franchise records. He is also tied for 16th in NFL history for touchdown catches. Ward had six seasons with more than 1,000 yards receiving. He was chosen for four Pro Bowls. Ward helped lead the Steelers to two Super Bowl victories.

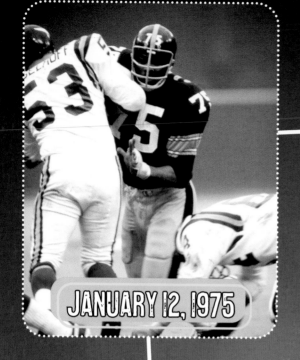

JANUARY 12, 1975

The Steelers collect their first championship in Super Bowl 9, defeating the Minnesota Vikings 16–6.

In Super Bowl 10, the Steelers defeat the Dallas Cowboys 21–17.

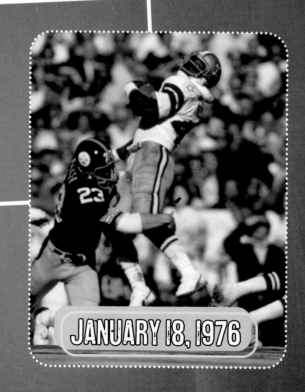

JANUARY 18, 1976

BIG DAYS

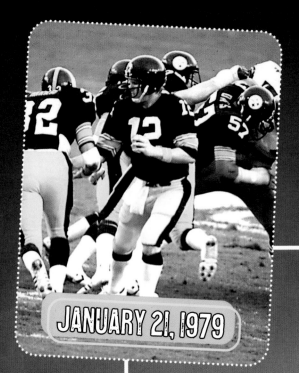

JANUARY 21, 1979

The Steelers again beat the Cowboys in Super Bowl 13 35–31. It's the first-ever Super Bowl rematch.

In Super Bowl 40, the Steelers defeat the Seattle Seahawks 21–10.

FEBRUARY 5, 2006

MODERN-DAY MARVELS

Minkah Fitzpatrick
Safety | Debut: 2019

The Steelers acquired Fitzpatrick in a trade with the Miami Dolphins in 2019. He had 11 interceptions in his first three NFL seasons, returning one interception for a touchdown in each of those seasons. He's been chosen for the Pro Bowl twice.

Najee Harris
Running Back | Debut: 2021

Harris starred at the University of Alabama before the Steelers selected him in the first round of the 2021 NFL Draft. A dual-threat to run with the football or catch passes, Harris totaled 1,667 yards as a rookie. He also scored a combined ten touchdowns in 2021. Harris's incredible rookie season was recognized with a trip to the Pro Bowl.

Ben Roethlisberger
Quarterback | Debut: 2004

Roethlisberger has led the Steelers to two Super Bowl victories. He's also quarterbacked the team to 165 regular season victories during his career. Roethlisberger has led the NFL in passing yards twice. He has been chosen for the Pro Bowl six times. Roethlisberger announced his retirement after the 2021 season.

T. J. Watt
Linebacker | Debut: 2017

Watt led the league with eight forced fumbles in 2019. Then he led the NFL with 15 **sacks** in 2020. After only five seasons in the league, he ranked fifth in Steelers history with 72 sacks. He was chosen for the Pro Bowl every season from 2018 to 2021.

"MEAN" JOE GREENE'S NICKNAME CAME FROM A NICKNAME GIVEN TO HIS COLLEGE FOOTBALL TEAM, THE NORTH TEXAS STATE UNIVERSITY MEAN GREEN.

JOE GREENE

"Mean" Joe Greene is considered one of the greatest defensive tackles ever to play the game of football. He was the anchor of the team's "Steel Curtain" defensive line, which was a major contributor to four Steelers Super Bowl victories. Greene was chosen for ten Pro Bowls. He is a member of the Pro Football Hall of Fame. Greene was also chosen for the NFL's 100th Anniversary All-Time Team.

#1

FAN FAVORITE

Jerome Bettis–Running Back
1996–2005

Jerome "The Bus" Bettis was beloved by fans for his bruising, powerful running style. He rushed for more than 1,000 yards during his first six seasons in Pittsburgh. He was chosen for six Pro Bowls. Bettis is also a member of the Pro Football Hall of Fame.

THE BIG GAME

FEBRUARY 1, 2009 – SUPER BOWL 43

The Steelers led the Arizona Cardinals for almost the entire game in Super Bowl 43. But with less than three minutes to go, Cardinals quarterback Kurt Warner found wide receiver Larry Fitzgerald. The long touchdown gave the Cardinals a 23–20 lead. Then it was quarterback Ben Roethlisberger's turn. He led the Steelers down the field and then found wide receiver Santonio Holmes. The six-yard touchdown pass gave the Steelers the lead with 35 seconds remaining in the game. They held on to win 27–23, and Holmes was named the game's MVP.

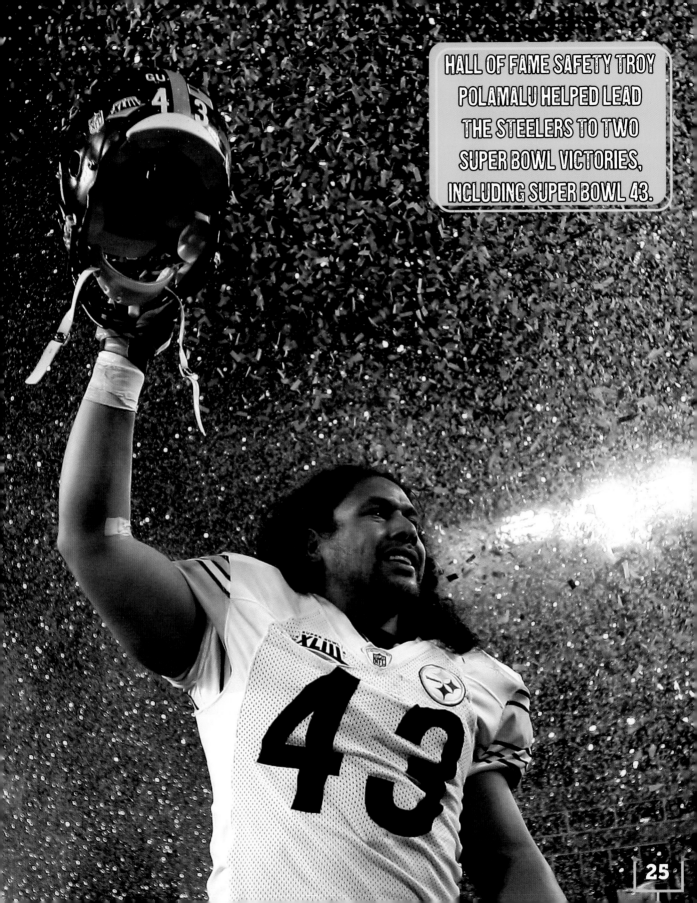

HALL OF FAME SAFETY TROY POLAMALU HELPED LEAD THE STEELERS TO TWO SUPER BOWL VICTORIES, INCLUDING SUPER BOWL 43.

MIKE TOMLIN HAS LED THE STEELERS TO MORE THAN 150 REGULAR SEASON VICTORIES AND ONE SUPER BOWL TITLE.

AMAZING FEATS

5,129 Passing Yards

In 2018 by **QUARTERBACK** Ben Roethlisberger

1,690 Rushing Yards

In 1992 by **RUNNING BACK** Barry Foster

136 Passes Caught

In 2015 by **WIDE RECEIVER** Antonio Brown

22.5 Sacks

In 2021 by **LINEBACKER** T. J. Watt

ALL-TIME BEST

PASSING YARDS

Ben Roethlisberger
64,880

Terry Bradshaw
27,989

Kordell Stewart
13,328

RUSHING YARDS

Franco Harris
11,950

Jerome Bettis
10,571

Willie Parker
5,378

RECEIVING YARDS

Hines Ward
12,083

Antonio Brown
11,207

John Stallworth
8,723

SACKS**

James Harrison
80.5

L. C. Greenwood
78

Joe Greene
77.5

SCORING

Gary Anderson
1,343

Jeff Reed
919

Chris Boswell
777*

INTERCEPTIONS

Mel Blount
57

Jack Butler
52

Donnie Shell
51

*as of 2021
**unofficial before 1982

LINEBACKER JAMES HARRISON PLAYED 14 SEASONS FOR THE STEELERS.

GLOSSARY

division (dih-VIZSH-un): a group of teams within the NFL who play each other more frequently and compete for the best record

Hall of Fame (HAHL of FAYM): a museum in Canton, Ohio, that honors the best players in NFL history

league (LEEG): an organization of sports teams that compete against each other

Most Valuable Player (MOHST VALL-yuh-bul PLAY-uhr): a yearly award given to the top player in the NFL

playoffs (PLAY-ahfs): a series of games after the regular season that decides which two teams play in the Super Bowl

Pro Bowl (PRO BOWL): the NFL's All-Star game where the best players in the league compete

rookie (RUH-kee): a player playing in his first season

sack (SAK): when a quarterback is tackled behind the line of scrimmage before he can throw the ball

stadium (STAY-dee-uhm): a building with a field and seats for fans where teams play

Super Bowl (SOO-puhr BOWL): the championship game of the NFL, played between the winners of the AFC and the NFC

touchdown (TUTCH-down): a play in which the ball is brought into the other team's end zone, resulting in six points

IN THE LIBRARY

Bulgar, Beth and Mark Bechtel. *My First Book of Football*.
New York, NY: Time Inc. Books, 2015.

Jacobs, Greg. *The Everything Kids' Football Book, 7th Edition*.
Avon, MA: Adams Media, 2021.

Sports Illustrated Kids. *The Greatest Football Teams of All Time*.
New York, NY: Time Inc. Books, 2018.

Wyner, Zach. *Pittsburgh Steelers*. New York, NY: AV2, 2020.

ON THE WEB

Visit our website for links about the Pittsburgh Steelers:
childsworld.com/links

Note to parents, teachers, and librarians: We routinely verify our web links to make sure they are safe and active sites. Encourage your readers to check them out!

ABOUT THE AUTHOR

Josh Anderson has published over 50 books for children and young adults. His two boys are the greatest joys in his life. Hobbies include coaching his sons in youth basketball, no-holds-barred games of Apples to Apples, and taking long family walks. His favorite NFL team is a secret he'll never share!